NOW YOU CAN READ...
Sleeping Beauty

STORY ADAPTED BY LUCY KINCAID

ILLUSTRATED BY GILLIAN EMBLETON

BRIMAX BOOKS • CAMBRIDGE • ENGLAND

A Princess had been born at the palace.

"We must make sure she has all a Princess should have," said the King. "We must invite the fairies to her christening."

"How many fairies live in our Kingdom?" asked the Queen. "Seven," said the King. "We must invite them all."
So the King sent invitations to each one. The King had seven golden caskets made as gifts for the seven fairies.

The day of the christening came. All the guests were sitting in the great palace hall. Suddenly the door flew open. Standing in the doorway was a very angry fairy.

"That is the fairy who lives at the bottom of the well," whispered the King. "I thought she had moved away. We did not send her an invitation."

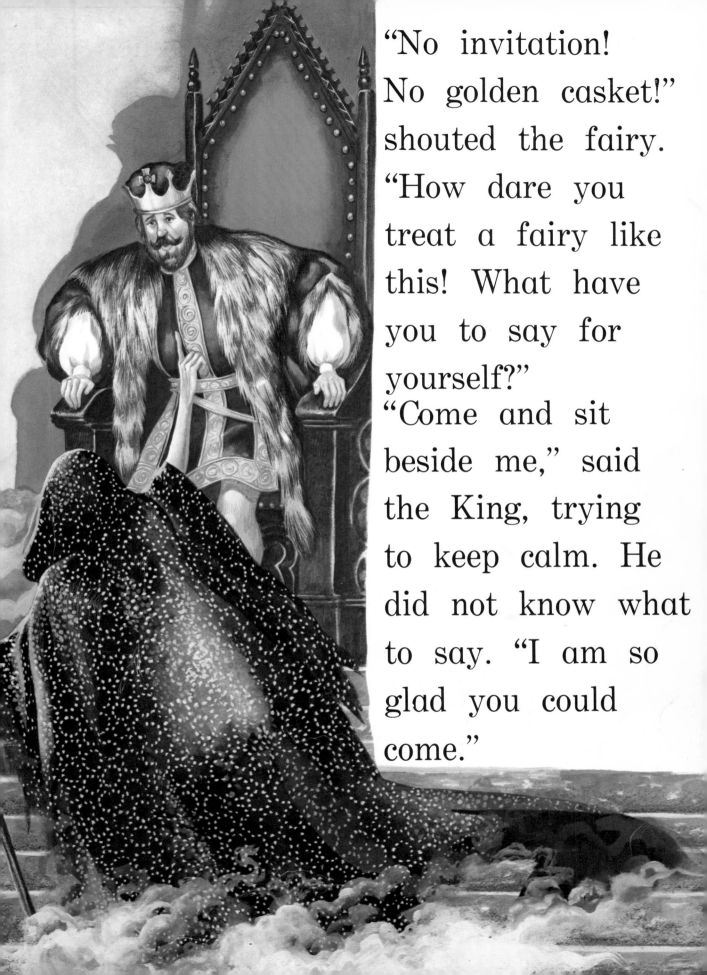

"No invitation! No golden casket!" shouted the fairy. "How dare you treat a fairy like this! What have you to say for yourself?"

"Come and sit beside me," said the King, trying to keep calm. He did not know what to say. "I am so glad you could come."

When the party was over, the
fairies stood round the cradle.
They had gifts for the baby
Princess.
It came to the seventh fairy's
turn to give the Princess a gift.
"Where is the seventh fairy?"
asked the King.
"Where is the seventh fairy?"
asked the Queen.
Nobody knew where she was.

"We cannot wait for her," said the fairy who had been forgotten. "I want to give my gift to the Princess." Everyone held his breath. Was she still angry?

"My gift shall be this," said the fairy with a sly smile. "The Princess shall prick her finger on a spindle and DIE!"

The King and Queen wept. Nobody knew what to do. It was then that the seventh fairy came back. "Do not weep," she said. "I too have a gift for the Princess. She will prick her finger it is true, but she will not die. She will sleep for one hundred years instead." Everyone went home. The Queen dried her tears. The Princess slept in her cradle.

The King ordered that all the spindles in the kingdom be destroyed. "If there are no spindles, the Princess cannot prick her finger on one," he said.

Sixteen years passed. One day the Princess went for a walk. She came to a tumbledown cottage. She pushed open the door and peeped inside. There was an old woman sitting by the window. She had a spindle in her hand. She was spinning thread. "Come along in," called the old woman.

"What are you doing?" asked the Princess.

"I am spinning," said the old woman.

The Princess watched the spindle twirl.

"Would you like to twirl the spindle?" asked the old woman.

"Yes please," said
the Princess. She
sat by the window
and took the spindle
from the old woman.
"Just a little
faster," said the
old woman.
"Like this?" said
the Princess.
"Faster . . . faster . . ."
said the old woman.

"Oh!" cried the Princess. "I have
pricked my finger." She fell to
the floor in a deep sleep. She
slept so soundly nobody could wake
her.

The seventh fairy heard what had happened to the poor Princess who was taken back to the palace and laid on her bed. The seventh fairy cast a spell that made everyone else in the palace sleep as soundly as the Princess.

"Now the Princess will not be alone when she wakes," said the fairy.

A thick, thorny hedge grew up round
the palace and hid it. The years
passed by. Strange stories were
told about what lay behind the hedge.
Many people tried to cut a way
through it, but nobody could.

One hundred years after the Princess had fallen asleep along came a Prince. The hedge seemed to melt at the touch of his sword. He could not believe what he saw. All over the palace there were people who had fallen asleep in the middle of what they had been doing.

There were cooks in the middle of cooking, maids in the middle of sweeping and pageboys in the middle of fighting. There were footmen in the middle of carrying messages, lords in the middle of talking and ladies in the middle of dressing. The Prince had to laugh.

When the Prince saw the sleeping Princess he kissed her. She opened her eyes and smiled at him. As she woke the palace clocks started ticking.

Then everyone else in the palace
woke too and carried on with what
they had been doing one hundred
years before. They all lived
happily ever after.

All these appear in the pages of the story. Can you find them?

King

Queen

Princess

cradle